Landforms

Caves

Cassie Mayer

Heinemann Library
Chicago, Illinois

© 2007 Heinemann Library
a division of Reed Elsevier Inc.
Chicago, Illinois

Customer Service   888–454–2279

Visit our website at www.heinemannlibrary.com

Photo research by Tracey Engel and Tracy Cummins
Designed by Jo Hinton-Malivoire
Printed and bound in China by South China Printing Company
11 10 09 08 07
10 9 8 7 6 5 4 3 2

Library of Congress Cataloging-in-Publication Data
Mayer, Cassie.
  Caves / Cassie Mayer.
    p. cm. — (Landforms)
  Includes bibliographical references and index.
  ISBN 1-4034-8434-1 (hc) — ISBN 1-4034-8440-6 (pb)
  ISBN 978-1-4034-8434-5 (hc) — ISBN 978-1-4034-8440-6 (pb)
  1. Caves—Juvenile literature. I. Title. II.Series.
  GB601.2.M39 2007
  551.44'7—dc22
                                2006004792
Acknowledgments
The author and publisher are grateful to the following for permission to reproduce copyright material:
Alamy pp. **6** (Chris Howes/Wild Places Photography), **11** (Chris Howes/Wild Places Photography), **22** (Simon Colmer and Abby Rex); Corel Professional Photos p. **13** (all); Corbis pp. **4** (river, Pat O'Hara; mountain, Royalty Free; volcano, Galen Rowell; island, George Steinmetz), **5** (Layne Kennedy), **7** (Tim Wright), **10** (Bob Krist), **12** (Richard T. Nowitz), **14** (P. van Gaalen/zefa), **15** (Tom Bean), **17** (David Muench), **18** (Eric and David Hosking), **19** (Wolfgang Kaehler), **20** (Danny Lehman), **21** (Annie Griffiths Belt), **23** (both, Richard T. Nowitz); Getty Images pp. **8** (Brian Bailey), **22** (Stephen Alvarez); Superstock pp. **9** (age footstock); **16** (SuperStock, Inc.).

Cover photograph of the stalagmites in Carlsbad Caverns' Big Room reproduced with permission of Corbis/George H. H. Huey. Backcover image of a sandstone cave reproduced with permission of Corbis/David Muench.

Every effort has been made to contact copyright holders of any material reproduced in this book. Any omissions will be rectified in subsequent printings if notice is given to the publisher.

Contents

Landforms

The land is made of different shapes.
These shapes are called landforms.

cave

A cave is a landform.
A cave is not living.

What Is a Cave?

A cave is an opening in the earth.

Caves are very dark.
Caves are made of rock.

Caves can be under the ground.

Caves can be in a hillside.

Caves can be big.

Caves can be small.

Features of a Cave

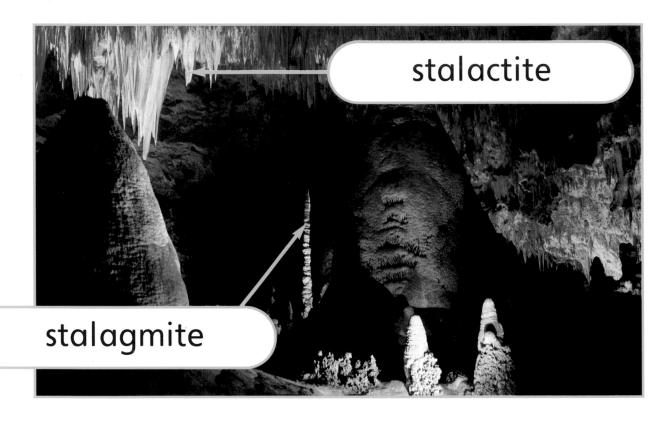

stalactite

stalagmite

Caves have many features.

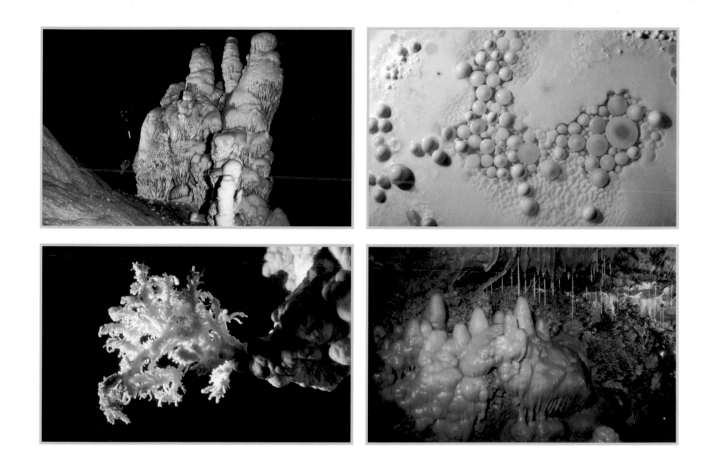

Cave features come in many sizes.
Cave features come in many shapes.

Types of Caves

Some caves are near the ocean.

Some caves are made of ice.

Most caves are made of rock.

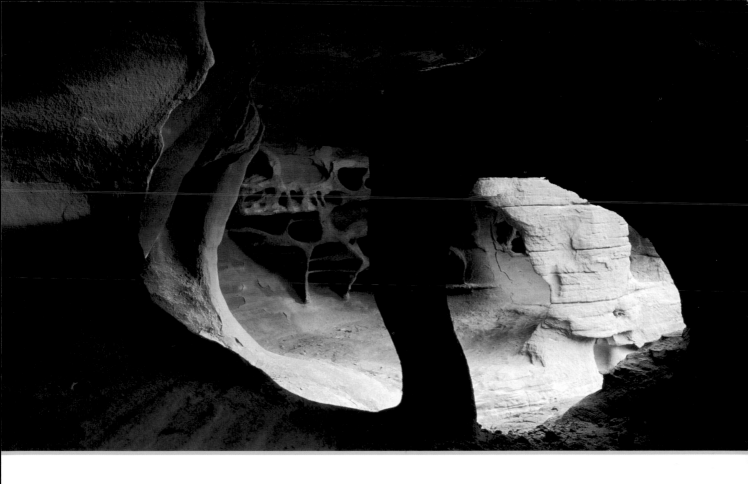

This cave is made of rock.
The rock is made of sand.

What Lives in a Cave?

bat

Caves are home to living things.
Animals live in caves.

People live in caves, too.

Visiting Caves

Many people like to visit caves.

Many caves show us hidden worlds.

Cave Facts

Mammoth Cave is in Kentucky. It is the largest group of caves in the world.

Some cave animals are blind. These animals have a good sense of touch.

Picture Glossary

stalactite a pointy shape on the ceiling of a cave

stalagmite a pointy shape on the floor of a cave

Index

Note to Parents and Teachers
This series introduces children to the concept of landforms as features that make up the earth's surface. Discuss with children landforms they are already familiar with, pointing out different landforms that exist in the area in which they live.

In this book, children explore the characteristics of caves. The photographs draw children in to the hidden world of caves and support the concepts presented in the text. The text has been chosen with the advice of a literacy expert to enable beginning readers success reading independently or with moderate support. An expert in the field of geology was consulted to ensure accurate content. You can support children's nonfiction literacy skills by helping them use the table of contents, headings, picture glossary, and index.